NEW HYMNS FOR THE LECTIONARY

NEW HYMNS
FOR THE LECTIONARY
To Glorify the Maker's Name

Music by Carol Doran
Words by Thomas H. Troeger

New York   Oxford
OXFORD UNIVERSITY PRESS
1986

Oxford University Press

Oxford   New York   Toronto
Delhi   Bombay   Calcutta   Madras   Karachi
Petaling Jaya   Singapore   Hong Kong   Tokyo
Nairobi   Dar es Salaam   Cape Town
Melbourne   Auckland

and associated companies in

Beirut   Berlin   Ibadan   Nicosia

Published by Oxford University Press, Inc.,
200 Madison Avenue, New York, New York 10016

Oxford is a registered trademark of Oxford University Press

Library of Congress Cataloging-in-Publication Data

Doran, Carol.
New hymns for the lectionary.

Includes indexes.
1. Hymns, English. I Troeger, Thomas H.,
1945–   . II. Title. III. Title: To glorify the
Maker's name.
M2117.D64N5   1986   85-755176
ISBN 0-19-385729-4 (alk. paper)

For M. and M. M.

Printing (last digit):   9 8 7 6 5 4 3 2 1

Printed in the United States of America
on acid-free paper

Introduction

We seek to blend the best qualities of traditional hymnody with a contemporary style that is not faddish or folksy. Each hymn in this collection explores a biblical text from the new ecumenical lectionary in words and music meant to draw the congregation closer to its meaning. Because the lectionary covers a great breadth of Scripture, these hymns embrace a wide range of Christian faith and pastoral need. There are hymns about the wonder and mystery of the incarnation, hymns that retell familiar Bible stories in dramatic form, hymns of healing, hymns for a heart brimming with praise, hymns for people seeking faith, hymns to stir people to action, hymns to bring comfort. Each is an effort to be true to the essential spirit of the Scripture in light of our own time and place in history.

Helpful Features

The collection has a number of features to help pastors and church musicians plan the introduction of new hymns to the congregation:

- The texts are written to traditional meters, so they may also be sung to traditional tunes.
- The melodies are written for easy unison singing; the keyboard accompaniments reinforce and amplify the sense and feeling of the words.
- The recollection of congregations singing with full attention to God and high satisfaction in singing together has shaped the keyboard accompaniments in this collection. Taking into account the fact that a group needs to hear itself singing, we assume an unrushed tempo and in many places have subdivided the main beats so that an energetic pulse may be evident even when the tempo is not fast.
- There are five indexes in the back to help you identify precisely the hymn you need:

Metrical Index
Scriptural Index

- The Index by Theme and Image features not only traditional topics but also a number of categories not usually found in hymnals, such as doubt, fearfulness in the presence of God, idolizing the past, opening ourselves to God.

- Finally, many of the hymns, though based on particular biblical lessons, will be appropriate for general service use even when that text is not read during worship.

Creative Ways to Use This Book

For Meditation and Prayer

Hymns have long been a devotional source for the Christian life, and these new hymns have been created in light of that tradition. In many cases the hymns follow the pattern of three-step spiritual meditation that became popular in England in the seventeenth century:

> Memory
> Understanding
> Will

The opening verses recall the story from the Bible (*memory*). The middle verses explore the contemporary meaning of that story (*understanding*), and the final verse is often a prayer to live God's will in accordance with what has been remembered and understood (*will*). For example, "Silence! Frenzied, Unclean Spirit" first retells the story of Jesus exorcising a demon, then probes the meaning of demons today, and concludes with a prayer for wholeness. This spiritual unfolding of the passage is highlighted by the music, which moves from percussive repetition into a songful melody that heralds Christ's healing power. Of course, not every hymn follows the pattern that strictly, but there is a fundamental meditative structure to nearly all of them that can assist individuals or a congregation in becoming spiritually centered.

For Preaching

Because these hymns are developed from particular biblical texts, they can be a resource for awakening a preacher's imaginative thinking about the scriptural passage. Recent homiletical theory has stressed the importance of story telling. Many of these hymns can help a preacher crystallize a clear narrative outline for a sermon. Even if the preacher arrives at a different interpretation of the scriptural passage, the poem may suggest images that can bring fresh life to a sermon.

Singing the hymn before the sermon can draw people into the biblical story, or singing it afterward can give the congregation an opportunity to respond to what has been preached. Used this way, the hymns will become an integrated part of the proclamation of the word of God.

For enriching and developing worship

Many of these hymns can be appropriately matched with special acts of worship such as weddings, funerals, and ordinations. (See the Index by Theme and Image.) Other hymns may suggest ways of enriching or even developing liturgical forms. For example, one could build a service around the hymns that explore different images of God and Christ. A service whose theme is peace might draw its structure from the hymn "The Sails Were Spilling Wind," in which there is a clear movement from Christ's bringing peace in the gospel, to inward peace, to international peace, to a prayer for making one's whole life a witness for peace. One could develop a series of sermons and services around the hymns based on biblical characters listed in the index. A church could heighten attention to the liturgical year and the use of the new lectionary by using the Index of Hymns in Sequence for the Liturgical Year. If a new hymn every week is too much for your congregation, the choir or soloists might offer the hymn for their anthem. If the hymn has a refrain, the choir can do the stanzas and the congregation can sing the refrain.

All of this is merely suggestive of the variety of ways in which this hymn book can be used. The principle to remember is that people are more open to new hymns when there is a sound theological and liturgical basis for their use. Then the hymn is more than an innovation; it is a coherent part of the service which is supported by all the surrounding elements of worship. At the same time, the new hymn can provide a fresh sense of the Spirit to renew and strengthen what is traditional.

How to Introduce These Hymns to a Congregation

The musician who leads the congregation in singing should precede the introduction of these hymns with a period of careful self-preparation. The accompaniment of congregational song requires steady and secure playing by the instrumentalist and thorough knowledge of the text and the music. In addition, the genuine enthusiasm you have developed during your study and practice of the new composition must be transmitted by your whole body when you stand before the people to teach a new hymn.

Here is a step-by-step process for introducing a new hymn:

1. If there is a choir or a small group of singers available to assist in the teaching, take adequate time to work with them on the new selection. Observing the points at which this smaller group has difficulty learning the music will help you to identify the places that will be challenging to the congregation.

2. In preparation for the presentation to the congregation, choose a limited portion to discuss which holds special interest or special difficulty for singers.

3. Stand before the people, and begin your presentation with a sentence or two about the overall nature of the hymn.

4. Mention the unusual section and play it (or have the small group sing it).

5. Invite the congregation to sing it.

6. Repeat the demonstration if the congregation has not been able to sing it well, and have them try singing it again.

It is important to have them succeed in singing the challenging section before ending this rehearsal, for they should be able to sing the hymn in its entirety during the worship service without the distractions of a sense of insecurity at the point of rhythmic notation or a melodic interval that is difficult to read.

If there is no small group within the congregation that is able to assist in introducing new music, or if the music leader has no opportunity to teach the people, it may be possible to introduce the tune by playing it several times as a prelude to the service, adding brief interludes between repetitions.

The authority with which the hymn is given out at the time the congregation sings it is greatly significant in the introduction of any new hymn. Secure and steady playing using expressive organ registration or piano technique is essential. Soloing out the melody will both clarify its contours and allow those who are preparing to sing the melody to hear the instrument's lyrical presentation as an example.

Acknowledgments

We have tested these hymns with a number of congregations and groups, and we are grateful for their willingness to give themselves—heart, soul, mind, and voice—to singing these new songs of faith. We want to thank the many chapters of the American Guild of Organists, who have invited us to lead workshops featuring our hymns; the Hymn Society of America, who gave us an opportunity to present many of these hymns at their 1984 Convocation; the Academy of Homiletics, which has used our Advent and Christmas hymns at their annual meetings; the First Presbyterian Church of Delaware, Ohio, and its pastor, Larry Hickle, who have tested a number of texts and tunes; the Central New York Conference of the United Church of Christ, who asked us to lead a workshop using both our hymns and the spiritual discipline by which we created them; the Downtown United Presbyterian Church of Rochester, New York, and especially their director of music, J. Melvin Butler, who has featured the Lenten hymns in a special service and given us great encouragement in the development of the book; the Auburn Seminary Continuing Education Seminars, which invited us to lead a series of workshops on revitalizing workshop and music in the local church; the Episcopal Bishops of Province II, who explored with us the theological and liturgical principles of our hymn writing; the Utica Presbytery, which used a cross-section of these hymns at a workshop on worship renewal; the Faculty Conference of the American Baptist Seminaries, which blended these hymns with reflections on their own religious history; and our own congregation at Colgate Rochester Divinity School/Bexley Hall/Crozer Theological Seminary, along with our Roman Catholic affiliate school, St. Bernard's Institute—a theological community whose diversity has helped us make this book ecumenical.

Writing for congregations with particular needs has often fueled our imaginations for the entire project, and we are indebted to a number of individuals and groups who have commissioned some of the hymns and settings in this book. The following hymns were initially written for these people: "Wind Who Makes All Winds That Blow"—Father Sebastian Falcone, director of St. Bernard's Institute, for a mass celebrating the gift of the Holy Spirit; "Praise to the Spinner Who Twisted and Twirled"—Leona Irsch, for her ordination to the deaconate of the Episcopal Church; "O Praise the Gracious Power"—Judith Ray, for her ordination as a teaching elder in the Presbyterian Church; "Listen to the Cloud That Brightens"—the Episcopal Diocese of Rochester, for the retirement of Bishop Robert Spears; "A Star Not Mapped on Human Charts"—the Rev. Richard L. Manzelmann, who wanted a new hymn about the wisemen and the star; the musical setting "Seminaries"—Larry Greenfield, for a service marking the fiftieth anniversary of our seminary campus; and the musical setting "Fisk"—the Downtown United Presbyterian Church of Rochester, New York, for the dedication of its new organ.

We are grateful as well to the journals that first published several of these hymns: *The American Baptist* ("Startled by a Holy Humming" and "The Word of God Was from the Start," December 1982); *The Christian Ministry* ("Wild the Man and Wild the Place," November 1982, "A Star Not Mapped on Human Charts," January 1983, "No Iron Spike, No Granite Weight," March 1983, "Wind Who Makes All Winds That Blow," May 1983, and "To Those Who Knotted Nets of Twine," July 1983); *Word & Witness* ("A Spendthrift Lover Is the Lord," special Advent resource issue, 1983); and *Reformed Liturgy & Music* ("Seek Not in Distant, Ancient Hills," summer 1983).

Finally, we want to thank Professor Richard French of the Yale Institute of Sacred Music, who has served as our editorial consultant. His keen ear and attention to detail have helped us revise both texts and musical setting so that they are more effective expressions of faith and praise.

We have written this book for the people of God, and our hope is that in singing these hymns they will be filled with the Spirit and empowered to do justice, to show mercy, and to face all things knowing that

> The Love of our God which we breathe with each breath
> Is with us forever in life and in death.

Rochester, New York   C. D.
August 1984   T. H. T.

Contents

The Life of Faith

NEW HYMNS FOR THE LECTIONARY

1. O Praise the Gracious Power

(tune: Christpraise Ray)
S.M. with refrain

Thomas H. Troeger

Carol Doran

With sturdy conviction ($\quarternote$ = 126)

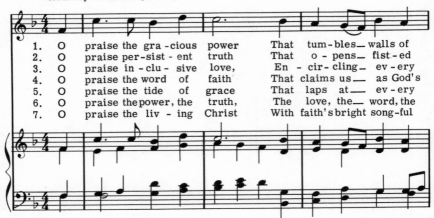

1. O praise the gra-cious power   That tum-bles_ walls of
2. O praise per-sist-ent truth   That o-pens_ fist-ed
3. O praise in-clu-sive love,   En-cir-cling_ ev-ery
4. O praise the word of faith   That claims us_ as God's
5. O praise the tide of grace   That laps at_ ev-ery
6. O praise the power, the truth,   The love, the_ word, the
7. O praise the liv-ing Christ   With faith's bright song-ful

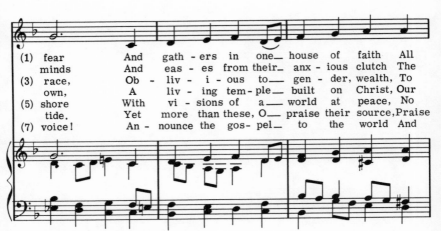

(1) fear   And gath-ers in one_ house of faith   All
    minds   And eas-es from their_ anx-ious clutch   The
(3) race,   Ob-liv-i-ous to_ gen-der, wealth, To
    own,   A liv-ing tem-ple_ built on Christ, Our
(5) shore   With vi-sions of a_ world at peace, No
    tide.   Yet more than these, O_ praise their source, Praise
(7) voice!   An-nounce the gos-pel_ to the world And

Text based on Ephesians 2: 11-22.

2

(1) stran - gers far and near:
prej - u - dice that blinds:
(3) so - cial rank or place:
rock and cor - ner - stone:
(5) long - er bled by war:
Christ the cru - ci - fied:
(7) with these words re - joice:

We praise you,

Christ! Your cross has made us one!

2. With Glad, Exuberant Carolings

(tune: Carol's Gift)
8-6-8-6-8-6

Thomas H. Troeger

Carol Doran

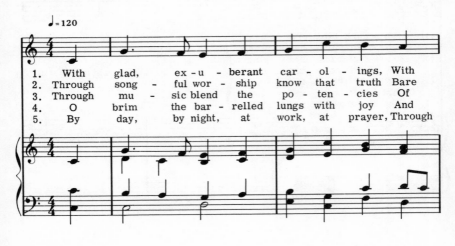

♩ = 120

1. With glad, ex-u-berant car-ol-ings, With
2. Through song-ful wor-ship know that truth Bare
3. Through mu-sic blend the po-ten-cies Of
4. O brim the bar-relled lungs with joy And
5. By day, by night, at work, at prayer, Through

(1) hymns and psalms of praise   Give thanks through Christ for
    words can-not en-fold.   In rap-tured mel-o-
(3) mind and heart and soul   And with their fu-sioned
    emp-ty out this song: "Our breath, our pulse, our
(5) storms and times of calm   Let all your deeds and

Text based on Ephesians 5: 15-20.

4

3. As a Chalice Cast of Gold

(tune: Inward Light)
7-7-7 D

Thomas H. Troeger

Carol Doran

1. As a chal - ice cast of gold,
2. Save me from the sooth - ing sin
3. When I bend up - on my knees,
4. When I dance or chant your praise,

(1) Burn-ished, bright and brimmed with wine,
    Of the emp - ty cul - tic deed
(3) Clasp my hands or bow my head,
    When I sing a psalm or hymn,

(1) Make me, Lord, as fit to hold Grace and
    And the pi - ous, bab - bling din Of the
(3) Let my spo - ken, pub - lic pleas Be di -
    When I preach your lov - ing ways, Let my

Text based on Mark 7: 1-8, 14-15, 21-23.

6

(1) truth and love di - vine.
claimed but un - lived creed.
(3) rect - ly, sim - ply said,
heart add its A - men.

(1) Let my praise and wor - ship start With the
Let my ac - tions, Lord, ex - press What my
(3) Free of tan - gled words that mask What my
Let each cher - ished, out - ward rite Thus re -

(1) cleans - ing of my heart.
tongue and lips pro - fess.
(3) soul would plain - ly ask.
flect your in - ward light.

for L. I. upon her ordination

4. Praise to the Spinner Who Twisted and Twirled

(tune: Wonderful Call)
10-11-11-12

Thomas H. Troeger   Carol Doran

1. Praise   to the spin-ner___ who   twist - ed and
2. Praise   to the weav-er___ whose mys - ti - cal
3. Praise   to the tai - lor___ whose nee - dle has
4. Spin - ner and Weav-er___ and Tai - lor of

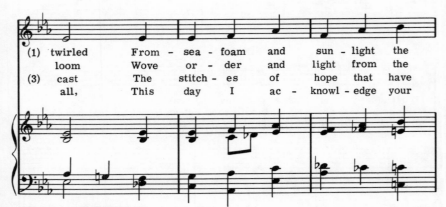

(1) twirled   From - sea - foam and sun - light the
     loom   Wove or - der and light from the
(3) cast   The stitch - es of hope that have
     all,   This day I ac - knowl - edge your

Text based on Psalm 104: 1-2.

     8

(1) life of this world. Those same nim - ble
cha - os and gloom. The shut - tle that
(3) held my heart fast; And bound as one
won - der - ful call, And ask through the

(1) fin - gers have gath - ered and fed My
tex - tured the night with the day Has
(3) fab - ric with - out an - y seams My
sac - ra - ments, wor - ship and prayer My

(1) joys and my sor - rows in - to faith's sin - gle thread.
wo - ven to - geth - er twines of grace with my clay.
(3) high - est, best vi - sions with the Spir - it's deep dreams.
life will make plain, Lord, it's your vest - ments I wear.

9

5. Unless This Day Be Holy

(tune: Lord's Day)
7-6-7-6 D

Thomas H. Troeger

Carol Doran

♩ =112

1. Un - less this day be ho - ly All
2. Our wor - ship, like the light - ning That
3. O let this day be ho - ly And

(1) days shall blur to one, As or - der - ly but
lifts the cur - tained night, Shall cast be - fore us
(3) rich in strength and peace, And when the day is

(1) emp - ty They march from sun to sun. But
shin - ing What dark - ness hides from sight: The
(3) o - ver Its mean - ing shall in - crease, As

Text based on Deuteronomy 5: 12-15.

10

(1) if we keep the Sab - bath
won - der and the glo - ry Through We
(3) day by day we la - bor To

(1) prayer and song and praise, We'll find the sa - cred
dim - ly sense and feel, The cir - cling sa - cred
(3) shape our work and art To fit the ho - ly

(1) mean - ing Of all our work - ing days.
pres - ence Our bus - y lives con - ceal.
(3) vis - ions That thun - der in our heart.

* A♮ would be appropriate for the final stanza.

11

6. What Fabled Names from Judah's Past

(tune: Eternal Name)
8-6-8-6-8-8

Thomas H. Troeger

Carol Doran

1. What fa - bled names from Ju - dah's past Did Mar - y's son re - ceive! But they whose lips these ti - tles cast Did
2. Some called him John while oth - ers said E - li - jah had re - turned. They ranked him with their treas - ured dead But
3. Then heav - en o - pened Pe - ter's mind And touched it with a flame, And while the Spir - it in him shined He
4. But Je - sus' words of pain and loss Caused Pe - ter to pro - test. He could not fit the nails and cross With
5. O Ris - en Sav - ior, keep us true To this our bold - est claim: In life and death we'll wor - ship you And

Text based on Mark 8: 27-35.

12

(1) not yet dare be - lieve:
none of them dis - cerned:
(3) spoke the Sav - ior's name: "You are the Christ! God's
what he had con - fessed:
(5) your e - ter - nal name:

ho - ly son, _____ Mes - si - ah,

Lord, A - noint - ed One! _____

7. Before the Temple's Great Stone Sill

(tune: Tenting Lord)
C.M.

Thomas H. Troeger

Carol Doran

1. Be - fore the tem - ple's great stone sill   Was
2. "Our tent - ing Lord who guides and calls   Has
3. If Na - than's words in - form our praise   And
4. But if we clutch with heart and hand   The
5. Grant, Lord, your church a tent - ing soul,   Not

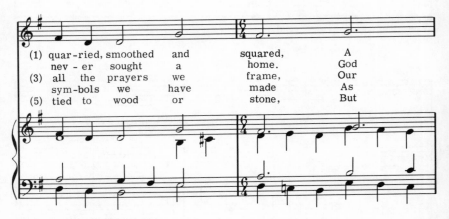

(1) quar - ried, smoothed and squared,   A
    nev - er sought a home.   God
(3) all the prayers we frame,   Our
    sym - bols we have made   As
(5) tied to wood or stone,   But

Text based on II Samuel 7: 1-17.

14

(1) dream - ing proph - et glimpsed God's will
will not be en - closed by walls.
(3) wor - ship then will leap and blaze
though they were God's first com - mand,
(5) fixed for - ev - er on this goal:

1, 2, 3, 4

(1) And heav-en's word de - clared.
God wants to move and roam."
(3) With God's con - fine - less flame.
Our prayer and song will fade.
(5) The praise of you a -

1, 2, 3, 4

5

(5) lone.

5

15

8. Too Splendid for Speech but Ripe for a Song

(tune: Carol's Vision)
10-10-11-11

Thomas H. Troeger

Carol Doran

Text based on Psalm 98.

16

(1) play To hon - or the pot - ter who made us from
spring Will teach us the lilt - ing new life we would
(3) noon God's play - ing and sing - ing a rav - ish - ing
bove, Are filled with the mu - sic of jus - tice and
(5) spire Will lead ev - ery na - tion to join in your

1, 3

(1) clay?

(3) tune.

2, 4   **5**

(2) sing.
(4) love.

(5) choir.

17

9. Crown As Your King

(tune: Fisk)
10-10-11-7, refrain 7-7-7-8

Thomas H. Troeger

Carol Doran

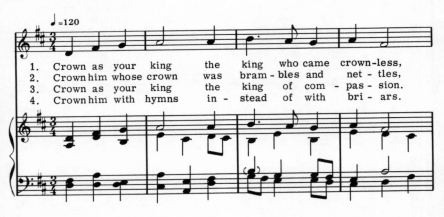

♩=120

1. Crown as your king the king who came crown-less,
2. Crown him whose crown was bram-bles and net-tles,
3. Crown as your king the king of com-pas-sion.
4. Crown him with hymns in-stead of with bri-ars.

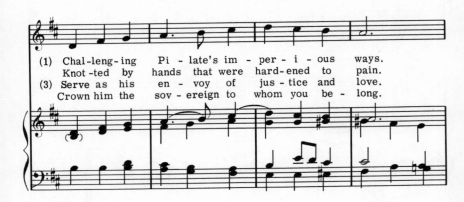

(1) Chal-leng-ing Pi-late's im-per-i-ous ways.
Knot-ted by hands that were hard-ened to pain.
(3) Serve as his en-voy of jus-tice and love.
Crown him the sov-ereign to whom you be-long.

Text based on John 18: 33 to 19: 5.

18

(1) Crown as your sov-ereign Christ whose love is bound-less.
Crown him whose gos-pel con - stant - ly un - set - tles
(3) Fill your com - mis - sion: faith - ful - ly re - fash - ion
Crown him with wor-ship. Braid with heav-en's choirs

(A)*   (A7)*

(1) Crown him with prayer and with praise!
Sys-tems of tyr - an -nous reign.
(3) Earth to the king - dom a - bove.
Gar-lands of mu - sic and song.

Refrain

Em - bla - zon up - on your heart The

*When introducing this tune, play a simple chordal accompaniment until the people are secure enough to sing the melody against the accompaniment which is written. The chords suggested for use during the learning period are not all compatible with the accompaniment provided for the hymn.

cross and the crim-soned crown,_____ The signs of your hum-ble king_____ Whose splen-did grace_____ the heav-ens sing.

10. Suddenly God's Sovereign Wind

(tune: Panaretos)
7-7-7 D

Thomas H. Troeger

Carol Doran

Sud-den-ly God's sov-ereign wind Rush-es down from heav-en's skies;

Love we can-not com-pre-hend Seiz-es us with

great sur-prise. Worlds be - yond this world of

Text based on John 3: 1-8.

21

broadening

sin Sweep us up: we're born a - gain!

Stanzas

1. Nic - o - de - mus tied and caught In a
2. Truth that danc - es past our reach, Like the
3. God re - lease us from our fear. Christ come

(1) web of cau - tious thought, In his need to keep con-
wind's loose leaf-tongued speech, Of - ten fills us with the
(3) close and hold us near. Wake in us a pure de-

(1) trol
fright
(3) sire
 And pro - tect his priv - ileged role,____
 Nic - o - de - mus felt that night____
 For your kiss, O Wind and Fire.____

(1) ——
——
(3) ——
 Could not stretch his mind to see
 When his heart and mind were torn
 Blow a - gain up - on this earth.
 How re -
 Hear - ing
 Give our

(1) birth could ev - er be.____
 he must be re - born.____
(3) trem - bling flesh re - birth.____

11. Wind Who Makes All Winds That Blow

(tune: Falcone)
7-7-7-7 D

Thomas H. Troeger

Carol Doran

1. Wind who makes all winds that blow—
2. Fire who fuels all fires that burn—
3. Ho - ly Spir - it, Wind and Flame,

(1) Gusts that bend the sap-lings low,
Suns a-round which plan-ets turn,
(3) Move with-in our mor-tal frame.

Gales that heave the
Bea - cons mark-ing
Make our hearts an

(1) sea in waves, Stir-rings in the mind's deep caves—
reefs and shoals, Shin-ing truth to guide our souls—
(3) al - tar pyre. Kin-dle them with your own fire.

Text based on Acts 2: 1-13.

(1) Aim your breath with stead - y power On your
Come to us as once you came: Burst in
(3) Breathe and blow up - on that blaze 'Til our

(1) church, this day, this hour. Raise, re - new the
tongues of sa - cred flame! Light and Pow - er,
(3) lives, our deeds and ways Speak that tongue which

ritard.

(1) life we've lost, Spir-it God of Pen - te - cost.
Might and Strength, Fill your church, its breadth and length.
(3) ev - ery land By your grace shall un - der-stand.

ritard.

25

12. A Spendthrift Lover Is the Lord

(tune: Spendthrift Lover)
C. M. D.

Thomas H. Troeger

Carol Doran

1. A spend-thrift lov-er is the Lord_____ Who nev-er
2. Still more is spent in blood and tears_____ To win the
3. How shall we love this heart-strong God_____ Who gives us

(1) counts the cost Or asks if heav-en can af-
   hu - man heart, To o-ver-come the vio - lent
(3) ev - ery-thing, Whose ways to us are strange and

(1) ford_____ To woo a world that's lost.
   fears_____ That drive the world a - part.
(3) odd,_____ What can we give or bring?

Text based on John 3: 14-21.

26

(1) Our lov - er toss - es coins of gold_____ A-cross the
Be-hold the bruised and thorn-crowned face_____ Of one who
(3) Ac-cept-ance of the match-less gift_____ Is gift e -

(1) mid - night skies And stokes the sun a - gainst the
bears our scars And emp-ties out the wealth of
(3) nough to give. The ver - y act will shake and

(1) cold_____ To warm us when we rise.
grace_____ That's hint-ed by the stars.
(3) shift_____ The way we love and live.

13. The Word of God Was from the Start

(tune: Logos)
L. M.

Thomas H. Troeger

Carol Doran

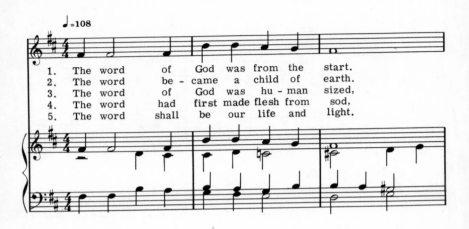

♩=108

1. The word of God was from the start.
2. The word be - came a child of earth.
3. The word of God was hu - man sized,
4. The word had first made flesh from sod,
5. The word shall be our life and light.

(1) The word drove seas and land a - part.
The word ar - rived through hu - man birth.
(3) The word by most un - rec - og - nized.
The word - made - flesh turned flesh toward God.
(5) The word shall be our power and might.

Text based on John 1: 1-14.

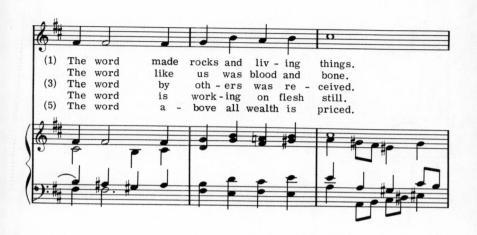

(1) The word   made   rocks and liv - ing   things.
    The word   like   us was blood and   bone.
(3) The word   by   oth - ers was re - ceived.
    The word   is   work - ing on flesh   still.
(5) The word   a - bove all wealth is   priced.

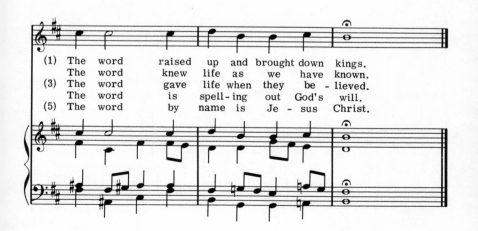

(1) The word   raised   up and brought down kings.
    The word   knew   life as   we   have known.
(3) The word   gave   life when they be - lieved.
    The word   is   spell - ing out God's   will.
(5) The word   by   name is Je - sus Christ.

14. The First Day of Creation

(tune: New Creation)
7-6-7-6-D

Thomas H. Troeger

Carol Doran

♩ = 126

1. The first day of cre - a - tion Is
2. Yet God is re - cre - at - ing More
3. All life in Christ is com - passed By

(1) dawn - ing in the soul, Up - on the deep God
than our in - ner world: Look up be - yond the
(3) that trans-form - ing grace Which spins new worlds and

(1) hov - ers Where fear and cha - os roll. The
plan - ets Where gal - ax - ies are swirled. Look
(3) won - ders In ev - ery time and place. O

Text based on II Corinthians 5: 6-10, 14-17 (esp. 17).

30

(1) in - ward dark is part - ing. The seas make
out and see how of - ten Sur - pris - ing
(3) Twirl - er of the star - dust, O Light no

(1) room for land. Great shore-lines are e -
love is shown. Christ is at work re -
(3) dark - ness rims, Your new cre - a - tion

(1) merg - ing A new world is at hand!
shap - ing Both stars and hearts of stone.
(3) pul - ses With wor - ship, praise and hymns.

31

15. Though Every Sun Shall Spend Its Fire

(tune: Light of Lights)
L. M.

Thomas H. Troeger

Carol Doran

1. Though ev-ery sun shall spend its fire
2. The Light of lights that danced and played
3. "Your ser-vant, Lord, let now de-part.
4. In us a-rise, O Light of lights,

(1) And gal-ax-ies shall dim to shade,
 In Sim-e-on's re-joic-ing face
(3) I've seen the Christ. In peace I go.
 Burn bright-ly in the cav-erned heart.

Text based on Luke 2: 22-40.

32

(1) The Light by whom these lights were made Shall nev - er
Shone through each word the old man prayed To realms be -
(3) What shines in heav - en shines be - low; Your light to
Con - sume the shade that fear sup-plies, And peace and

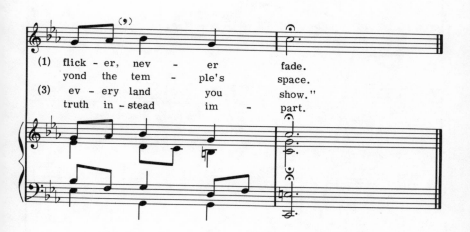

(1) flick - er, nev - er fade.
yond the tem - ple's space.
(3) ev - ery land you show."
truth in - stead im - part.

16. Gangling Desert Birds Will Sing

(tune: Lance)
7-7-7-7 D

Thomas H. Troeger

Carol Doran

1. "Gang-ling des - ert birds_____ will sing;
2. "In this strange and for - eign land
3. While the ex - iles far_____ from home
4. Lord, a - lert our eyes_____ to probe

(1) Jack - als too will join God's choir.
    God in un - ex - pect - ed ways
(3) Watched their cap-tors' mud - dy streams
    With I - sa - iah's deep-er sight

Riv - ers out of rock__
Will do mir - a - cles__
Pass be-tween flat banks__
Where to - day up - on__

(1)__ will spring;   Paths will cut through thorn and briar.
    __ as grand   As the an - cient deeds you praise.
(3)__ of loam   Zi - on's riv - ers filled their dreams
    __ this globe   You are sow - ing deeds of light.

Text based on Isaiah 43: 16-25. Also Psalm 137.

34

(1) In the wil - der - ness_____ of sand
God who pushed a - side_____ the sea
(3) 'Til I - sa - iah's words_____ of grace
Ease our yearn- ing for_____ the past

(1) God will lead us by the hand."
Still re - deems and sets us free."
(3) Thun-dered through that pa - gan place:
'Til we see by faith at last:
"Here and now, in

broadening

clear, plain view, God is do-ing some-thing new!"

broadening

35

17. God Folds the Mountains Out of Rock

(tune: Revision)
L. M. D.

Thomas H. Troeger

Carol Doran

Text based on Job 28.

(1) stone we lift up fire, And too im-pressed by our own skill
is the great-er need, And wis-dom is the great-er source,
(3) moun-tains rich-ly veined Will be a source of light and flame

(1) We use the flame that we ac-quire
For lack - ing wis - dom we pro - ceed
(3) Whose en - er - gies have been or - dained

(1) Not think - ing of the Mak - er's will.
To waste God's oth - er gifts on force.
(3) To glo - ri - fy the Mak - er's name.

18. The Lick of the Tide, the Lunge of the Storm

(tune: Faithful Love)
10-10-11-11

Thomas H. Troeger

Carol Doran

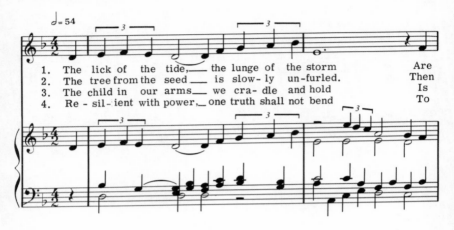

♩ = 54

1. The lick of the tide,— the lunge of the storm
2. The tree from the seed — is slow-ly un-furled.
3. The child in our arms— we cra-dle and hold
4. Re - sil - ient with power,— one truth shall not bend

Are
Then
Is
To

(1) shift-ing the beach— and chang-ing its form.
felt at its height— when light-ning is hurled.
(3) one day grown up— and one day grown old.
tide or to storm,— to light-ning or wind:

The
The
Each
The

Text based on Romans 8: 31-39.

38

(1) riv-ers and rains— are re-sculpt-ing the hill—
tow-er- ing wood— lies in ash on the earth,
(3) mus-cle and bone— knows the forc - es and strain
love of our God— which we breathe with each breath

But
But
That
Is

(1) no - thing's e - rod - ing the Lord's lov - ing will.
flame has not dam- aged the source of re-birth.
(3) lev - el high moun-tains to val - ley and plain.
with us for - ev - er in life and in

1, 2, 3,

death.

39

19. Startled by a Holy Humming

(tune: Annunciation)
8-7-8-7 D

Thomas H. Troeger

Carol Doran

1. Star - tled   by a ho - ly hum - ming
2. Troub - led   by the an - gel's bless - ing
3. Tend - ing   to the voice of heav - en
4. Start - led,   trou - bled, then be - liev - ing

(1) Drum - ming in her heart and ear,   Mar - y heard an an - gel
    Mar - y asked how it could be.   In a way she was con -
(3) Mar - y's doubts be - gan to fade   While her faith like ris - ing
    Mar - y's vi - sion o - pened wide.   She by faith be - gan per -

(1) com - ing,—   Ga - bri - el was draw - ing near.   From the
    fess - ing —   All that doubt could nev - er see: How the
(3) leav - en—   Grew un - til she glad - ly prayed: "May it
    ceiv - ing—   Life and truth from heav - en's side.   Lord, may

Text based on Luke 1: 26-38.

40

(1) loud though sound-less beat- ing___ Of the flash-ing, un - seen
flesh is filled with spir - it,___ How the heart can beat with
(3) be as God has spo -ken,___ May it be as I have
we at last like Mar - y ___ Catch the slant of heav-en's

(1) wings Pulsed the words of sa - cred greet-ing:___ She would
love, How an -oth - er heart can hear it,___ How this
(3) heard, May God's will be nev - er bro-ken,___ May I
light Pierc - ing through the doubts that bur - y ___ Hope and

1, 2, 3
(1) bear the king of kings.
comes from God a - bove.
(3) live by God's own word."
grace from hu - man

4
(4) sight.

Introduce this hymn by playing it all the way through, continuing *through* the first ending without pause. The people join in singing as the first line is again played.

20. The Sheep Stood Stunned in Sudden Light

(tune: Heaven's Tide)
L. M.

Thomas H. Troeger

Carol Doran

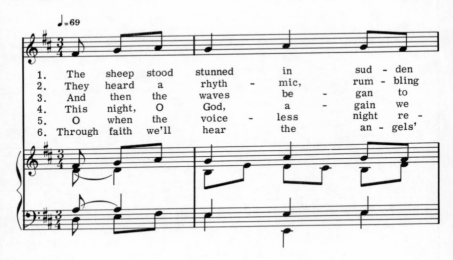

♩ = 69

1. The sheep stood stunned in sud - den
2. They heard a rhyth - mic, rum - bling
3. And then the waves be - gan to
4. This night, O God, a - gain we
5. O when the voice - less night re -
6. Through faith we'll hear the an - gels'

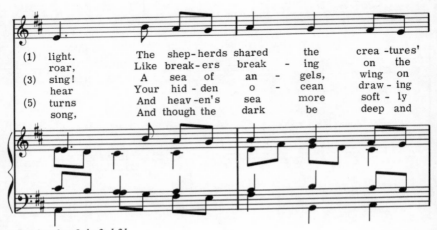

(1) light. The shep-herds shared the crea -tures'
    roar, Like break-ers break - ing on the
(3) sing! A sea of an - gels, wing on
    hear Your hid - den o - cean draw - ing
(5) turns And heav -en's sea more soft - ly
    song, And though the dark be deep and

Text based on Luke 2: 1-21.

(1) fright,   While heav - en's   star   em - broi - dered
     shore   And run - ning   up   the   thir - sty
(3) wing,   Was cir - cling, chant   ting   in   the
     near,   A - gain we   sense   through Je - sus'
(5) churns,   May faith be   like   the   shell   that
     long,   We'll brave - ly   live,   for   by   our

(1) train   Swept o - ver   hills and down   the   plain.
     strand   To toss a   treas-ure on   the   land.
(3) skies   The news of   Christ be - fore   their   eyes.
     birth   The sea of   grace that   cir - cles   earth.
(5) sends   The sound of   o - cean waves and   winds.
     side   Is Christ who   came on   heav - en's   tide.

21. The Hands That First Held Mary's Child

(tune: Father Moynihan)
C. M. D.

Thomas H. Troeger

Carol Doran

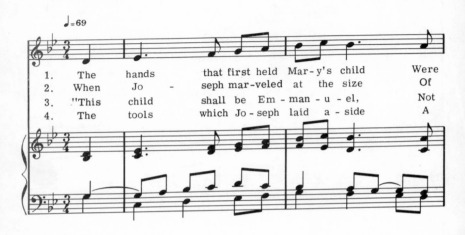

1. The hands that first held Mar-y's child Were
2. When Jo - seph mar-veled at the size Of
3. "This child shall be Em - man - u - el, Not
4. The tools which Jo - seph laid a - side A

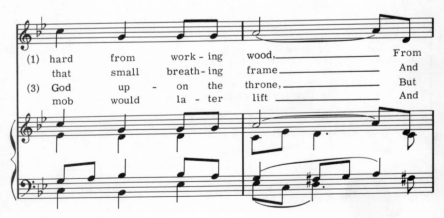

(1) hard from work - ing wood, From
that small breath-ing frame And
(3) God up - on the throne, But
mob would la - ter lift And

Text based on Matthew 1: 18-25.

44

(1) boards they sawed and planed and filed   And splin-ters
    gazed up - on those bright new eyes   And spoke the
(3) God with us, Em - man - u - el,   As close as
    use with an - ger, fear and pride   To cru - ci -

(1) they with - stood. ___   This day they gripped no
    in - fant's name, ___   The an-gel's words he
(3) blood and bone." ___   The ti - ny form in
    fy God's gift. ___   Let us, O Lord, not

(1) tool of steel,   They drove no i - ron nail, ___   But
    once had dreamed   Poured down from heav-en's height, ___   And
(3) Jo-seph's palms   Con-firmed what he had heard, ___   And
    on - ly hold   The child who's born to - day, ___   But

45

(1) cra - dled from the head to heel Our Lord, new -born and
like the host of stars that beamed Blessed earth with wel-come
(3) from his heart rose hymns and psalms For heav-en's hu - man
charged with faith may we be bold To fol - low in his

1, 3

(1) frail.

(3) word.

2, 4

(2) light.

(4) way.

* fine

* Observe fermatas for *fine* only.

46

22. A Cheering, Chanting, Dizzy Crowd

(tune: King's Welcome)
C. M.

Thomas H. Troeger

Carol Doran

1. A cheer-ing, chant-ing, diz-zy crowd Had
2. They laid their gar-ments in the road And
3. When day dimmed down to deep-ening dark The
4. Lest we be fooled be-cause our hearts Have
5. In-stead of palms a wind-ing sheet Will

(1) stripped the green trees bare, And hail-ing Christ as king a-
spread his path with palms And vows of last-ing love be-
(3) crowd be-gan to fade 'Til on-ly tram-pled leaves and
surged with pass-ing praise, Re-mind us, God, as this week
(5) have to be un-rolled, A car-pet much more fit to

(1) loud, Waved bran-ches in the air.
stowed With roy-al hymns and psalms.
(3) bark Were left from the pa-rade.
starts Where Christ has fixed his gaze.
(5) greet The king a cross will hold.

Text based on Mark 11: 1-11.

47

23. A Star Not Mapped on Human Charts

(tune: Star Divine)
C. M. D.

Thomas H. Troeger

Carol Doran

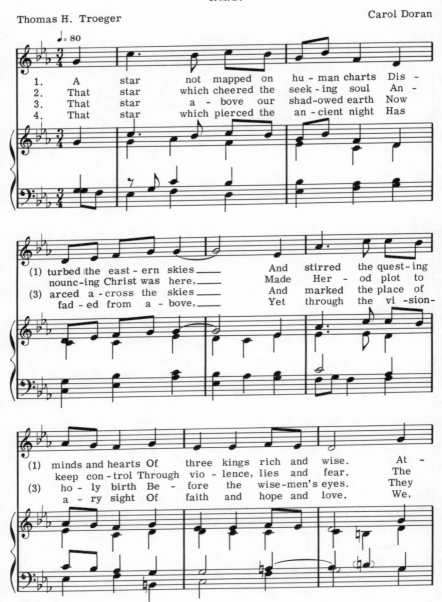

♩ = 80

1. A star not mapped on hu-man charts Dis-
2. That star which cheered the seek-ing soul An-
3. That star a-bove our shad-owed earth Now
4. That star which pierced the an-cient night Has

(1) turbed the east-ern skies____ And stirred the quest-ing
    nounc-ing Christ was here,____ Made Her - od plot to
(3) arced a-cross the skies____ And marked the place of
    fad-ed from a-bove,____ Yet through the vi-sion-

(1) minds and hearts Of three kings rich and wise. At-
    keep con-trol Through vio-lence, lies and fear. The
(3) ho - ly birth Be - fore the wise-men's eyes. They
    a - ry sight Of faith and hope and love. We,

Text based on Matthew 2: 1-12.

Text © 1983, Thomas H. Troeger
Music © 1985, Oxford University Press, Inc.

48

(1) tract-ed by the mys - tic light Their sci - ence did not
ty - rant hid his anx - ious thought And said, "Re -port to
(3) of -fered in - cense, myrrh and gold While on their knees to
like the wise-men, still may find Life's an - i - mat- ing

(1) frame, They trav - eled through the cloud of
me When you have found the child you've
(3) pray. Then through a dream the kings were
goal: The Christ who prompts the prob - ing

(1) night To learn its ho - ly name.
sought That I may come and see."
(3) told: "Go home an - oth - er way!"
mind And lights the o - pen soul.

49

24. The Scantest Touch of Grace Can Heal

(tune: Healing Grace)
C. M.

Thomas H. Troeger

Carol Doran

1. The scant-est touch of grace can heal A
2. Ob - serve a hand stretched out to brush The
3. She can - not see the sav - ior's face, But
4. Like her, O Christ, we reach for you. One

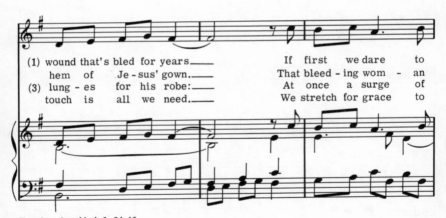

(1) wound that's bled for years____ If first we dare to
hem of Je - sus' gown.____ That bleed - ing wom - an
(3) lung - es for his robe:____ At once a surge of
touch is all we need.____ We stretch for grace to

Text based on Mark 5: 21-43.

(1) reach   and feel Be - yond our pain and   tears.
trusts   one touch Will make her bod - y
(3) heal - ing grace Where stub-born blood has   flowed.
make   us   new And   heal our wounds that

* D♯ may replace D in Stanzas 3 and 4.

(2) sound.

(4) bleed.

51

25. Silence! Frenzied, Unclean Spirit

(tune: Authority)
8-7-8-7 D

Thomas H. Troeger

Carol Doran

Text based on Mark 1: 21-28.

52

(1) fore the sun." At Christ's voice the demon trembled,
    grip and bind, Doubts that stir the heart to panic,
(3) shall depart. Clear our thought and calm our feeling,

(1) From its victim madly rushed, While the crowd that
    Fears distorting reason's sight, Guilt that makes our
(3) Still the fractured, warring soul. By the power

(1) was assembled Stood in wonder, stunned and hushed.
    loving frantic, Dreams that cloud the soul with fright.
(3) of your healing Make us faithful, true and whole.

* Play small notes for final stanza.

26. The Leper's Soul Was No Less Scarred

(tune: Leper's Soul)
C. M.

Thomas H. Troeger

Carol Doran

1. The lep-er's soul was no less scarred Than were his face and skin._____ The curse, "Un-clean, un-clean!" had marred God's im-age deep with-in.
2. No hands had grasped his hands for years, No lips had kissed his own,_____ No greet-ing came his way but jeers And looks of ice and stone.
3. Then Je-sus stroked the lep-er's cheek And swept the sores a-way_____ But charged the man he should not speak Of what took place that day.
4. There was, of course, no way to hold The news of what Christ did._____ The man made sure the tale was told In-stead of hushed and hid.
5. And we who feel Christ's heal-ing hand Can't help but do the same._____ The way we speak and walk and stand Will spell our sav-ior's name.

Text based on Mark 1: 40-45.

54

27. Soundless Were the Tossing Trees

(tune: Soundless)
7-7-7-7 D

Thomas H. Troeger

Carol Doran

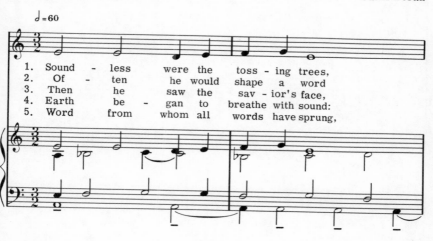

1. Sound - less were the toss - ing trees,
2. Of - ten he would shape a word
3. Then he saw the sav - ior's face,
4. Earth be - gan to breathe with sound:
5. Word from whom all words have sprung,

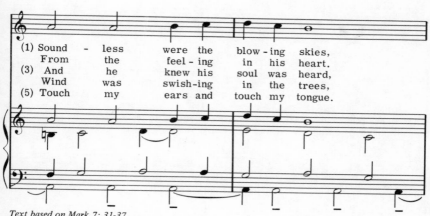

(1) Sound - less were the blow - ing skies,
From the feel - ing in his heart.
(3) And he knew his soul was heard,
Wind was swish-ing in the trees,
(5) Touch my ears and touch my tongue.

Text based on Mark 7: 31-37.

(1) Sound - less   were the   driv - en leaves—
Risk - ing   what he   nev - er heard,
(3) Knew   that   Christ with ten - der grace
Leaves   were   rat - tling   on the ground,
(5) Clear   the   pas - sage   to my heart.

(1) Sound -less all   be - fore the   eyes
Pull - ing both   his   lips a - part,
(3) Did   not find   his   groans ab - surd,
Chil - dren shout - ed,   gig - gled, teased
(5) Speak with - in   my   in - ward part.

(1) Of   a   man   who   ev - ery day   Watched the
Blow - ing hard,   he   tried to reach   Oth - er
(3) Knew as   Je - sus   drew him near   Not   to
'Round the sing - ing,   splash-ing well   Near the
(5) Let your voice   as   thun - der roll   Down   the

56

(1) sound - less chil - dren play 'Round the
  peo - ple's world of speech, Though the
(3) flinch a - way in fear, But to
  toll - ing, ring - ing bell. He could
(5) can - yons of my soul 'Til your

(1) sound - less, splash - ing well Near the
  sounds he cast in air Of - ten
(3) trust his prob - ing hand And to
  hear, O he could hear! And his
(5) word re - turns to you, Ech - o -

(1) sound - less vil - lage bell.
  brought a baf - fled stare.
(3) read his lips' com - mand.
  speech was pure and clear!
(5) ing in all I do.

28. We Have the Strength to Lift and Bear

(tune: Healing Power)
C. M. D.

Thomas H. Troeger

Carol Doran

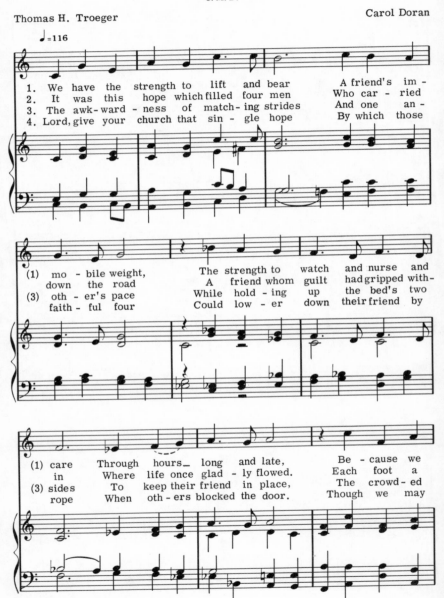

1. We have the strength to lift and bear A friend's im-
2. It was this hope which filled four men Who car - ried
3. The awk - ward - ness of match - ing strides And one an -
4. Lord, give your church that sin - gle hope By which those

(1) mo - bile weight, The strength to watch and nurse and
   down the road A friend whom guilt had gripped with-
(3) oth - er's pace While hold - ing up the bed's two
   faith - ful four Could low - er down their friend by

(1) care Through hours_ long and late, Be - cause we
   in Where life once glad - ly flowed. Each foot a
(3) sides To keep their friend in place, The crowd - ed
   rope When oth - ers blocked the door. Though we may

Text based on Mark 2: 1-12.

58

(1) trust   in ways   un - known   The   springs of
     stone,   each leg   a   rod,   For   years he
(3) street,   the roof   of   clay,   The scribe's harsh
     lack   your gift   to   heal,   This   task   is

(1) health are stirred,   And thus the   mind, the flesh and
     lay in bed,   In ter - ror   of   a   judg-ing
(3) view of sin—   Not all of   these could turn a -
     sure - ly ours: To bring to   you the lost who

(1) bone   Re - ceive Christ's heal - ing   word.
     god   And par - a - lyzed   by   dread.
(3) way   Those stub - born lov - ing   men.
     feel   Their need of   gra - cious powers.

29. If Christ Is Charged with Madness

(tune: Heaven's Madness)
7-6-7-6 D

Thomas H. Troeger

Carol Doran

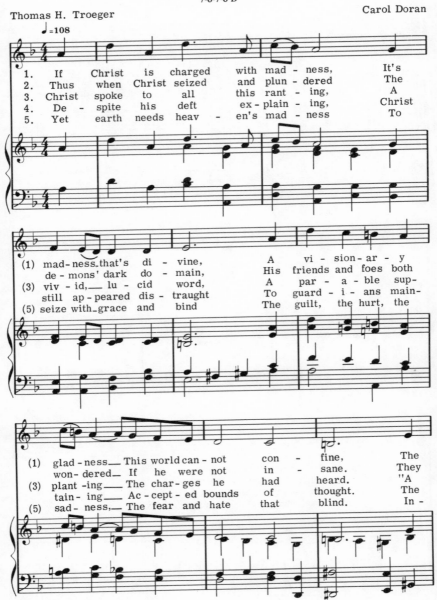

Text based on Mark 3: 20-35.

60

(1) mad - ness of con - ceiv - ing What
charged his soul was riv - en, His
(3) house that is di - vid - ed, A
force of faith in ac - tion Seems
(5) trude, O Christ, im - pas - sioned With

(1) no one else can see, Then act - ing and be -
heart and mind pos - sessed By for - ces he had
(3) king - dom, soul or land With rag - ing wars in - re
mad - ness to each age And of - ten the re -
(5) mad - ness that's di - vine Up - on the world we've

rit.

(1) liev - ing So it will come to be.
driv - en From those who were dis - tressed.
(3) side it Can - not sur - vive and stand."
ac - tion Is fear dis - guised as rage.
(5) fash - ioned And give it your de - sign.

rit.

61

30. Far from the Markets of Rich Meat and Wine

(tune: Simple Meal)
10-10-10-10

Thomas H. Troeger

Carol Doran

♩=120

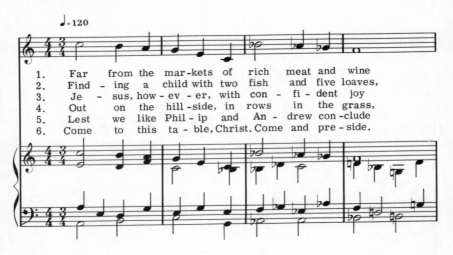

1. Far from the mar-kets of rich meat and wine
2. Find - ing a child with two fish and five loaves,
3. Je - sus, how - ev - er, with con - fi - dent joy
4. Out on the hill -side, in rows in the grass,
5. Lest we like Phil - ip and An - drew con -clude
6. Come to this ta - ble, Christ. Come and pre - side.

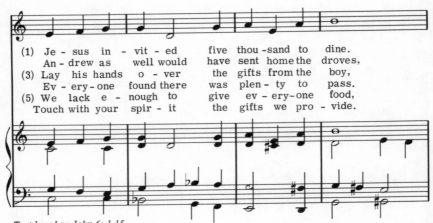

(1) Je - sus in - vit - ed five thou -sand to dine.
    An - drew as well would have sent home the droves,
(3) Lay his hands o - ver the gifts from the boy,
    Ev - 'ery-one found there was plen - ty to pass.
(5) We lack e - nough to give ev - 'ery-one food,
    Touch with your spir - it the gifts we pro - vide.

Text based on John 6: 1-15.

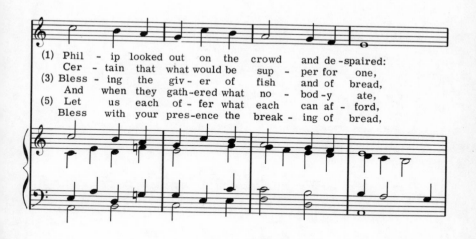

(1) Phil - ip looked out on the crowd and de -spaired:
Cer - tain that what would be sup - per for one,
(3) Bless - ing the giv - er of fish and of bread,
And when they gath -ered what no - bod -y ate,
(5) Let us each of - fer what each can af - ford,
Bless with your pres-ence the break - ing of bread,

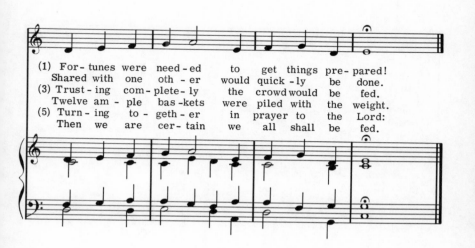

(1) For- tunes were need - ed to get things pre- pared!
Shared with one oth - er would quick -ly be done.
(3) Trust - ing com- plete- ly the crowd would be fed.
Twelve am - ple bas -kets were piled with the weight.
(5) Turn - ing to -geth - er in prayer to the Lord:
Then we are cer - tain we all shall be fed.

63

31. The Sails Were Spilling Wind

(tune: Bürklin)
6-6-6-6-8-8

Thomas H. Troeger

Carol Doran

1. The sails were spill - ing wind, The
2. The sea be - came a glass, Re -
3. Then head - ing toward the land, They
4. The storm re - turns a - gain. In
5. This war - ring world shall end Un -
6. Through ev - ery act and word Of

(1) boat was tak - ing waves. ___ The mast be - gan to
   flect - ing heav - en's light. ___ The storm com-plete - ly
(3) mar - veled on the way ___ That Je - sus could com-
   ev - ery heart it raves ___ Un - til we hear a -
(5) less we make it clear ___ The One who tamed the
   all our liv - ing days ___ May Christ's own voice be

Text based on Mark 4: 35-41.

64

REFRAIN:

(1) bend.   Then called the Lord   who   saves:
    passed   When Je - sus said   that night:
(3) mand   And   make the sea   o - bey: "Be
    gain   The   Lord who told   the   waves:
(5) wind   Can   tame our hate   and   fear:
    heard   Un - til the world   o - beys:

Peacefully (♩ =68)

still,_____ be still,_____ and rage no more!_____

_____ Let peace de - scend on sea   and   shore."

65

32. No Iron Spike, No Granite Weight

(tune: Lemke)
L. M.

Thomas H. Troeger

Carol Doran

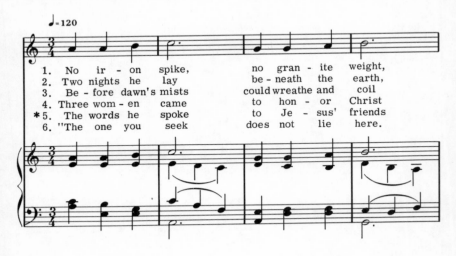

1. No ir-on spike, no gran-ite weight,
2. Two nights he lay be-neath the earth,
3. Be-fore dawn's mists could wreathe and coil
4. Three wom-en came to hon-or Christ
*5. The words he spoke to Je-sus' friends
6. "The one you seek does not lie here.

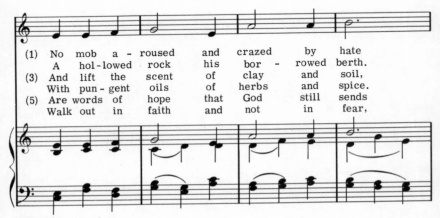

(1) No mob a-roused and crazed by hate
    A hol-lowed rock his bor-rowed berth.
(3) And lift the scent of clay and soil,
    With pun-gent oils of herbs and spice.
(5) Are words of hope that God still sends
    Walk out in faith and not in fear,

* Verse 5 is optional.
Text based on Mark 16: 1-8.

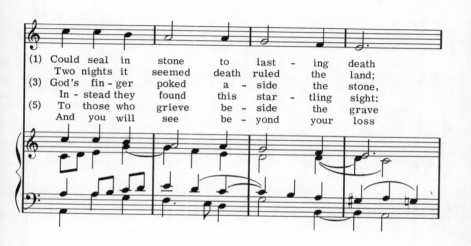

(1) Could seal in stone to last - ing death
Two nights it seemed death ruled the land;
(3) God's fin - ger poked a - side the stone,
In - stead they found this star - tling sight:
(5) To those who grieve be - side the grave
And you will see be - yond your loss

(1) The Christ who is our life and breath.
Two nights and then death lost com - mand.
(3) And Christ a - rose to take his throne.
A young man sit - ting robed in white.
(5) And ask if God can real - ly save:
To Christ who lives de - spite the cross. "

33. These Things Did Thomas Count As Real

(Tune: Merle Marie)
L. M.

Thomas H. Troeger

Carol Doran

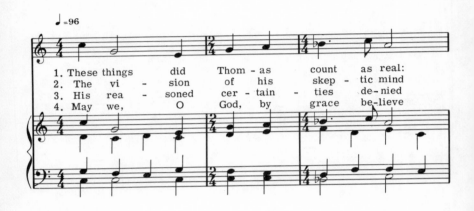

♩ =96

1. These things did Thom - as count as real:
2. The vi - sion of his skep - tic mind
3. His rea - soned cer - tain - ties de - nied
4. May we, O God, by grace be-lieve

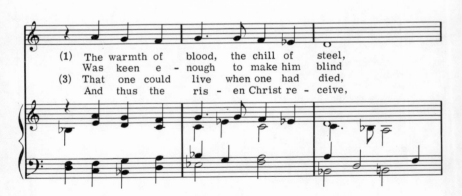

(1) The warmth of blood, the chill of steel,
Was keen e - nough to make him blind
(3) That one could live when one had died,
And thus the ris - en Christ re - ceive,

Text based on John 20: 19-31.

68

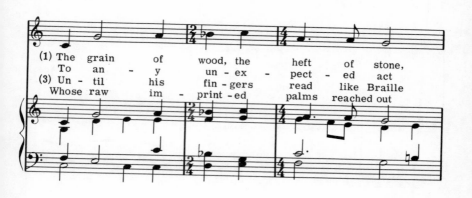

(1) The grain of wood, the heft of stone,
    To an - y un - ex - pect - ed act
(3) Un - til his fin - gers read like Braille
    Whose raw im - print - ed palms reached out

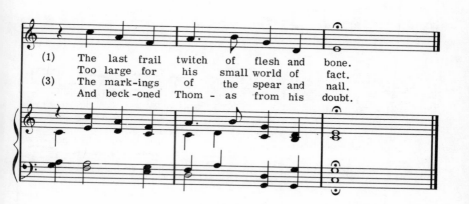

(1) The last frail twitch of flesh and bone.
    Too large for his small world of fact.
(3) The mark-ings of the spear and nail.
    And beck-oned Thom - as from his doubt.

34. The Love That Lifted Lyric Praise

(tune: David's Song)
L. M. D.

Thomas H. Troeger

Carol Doran

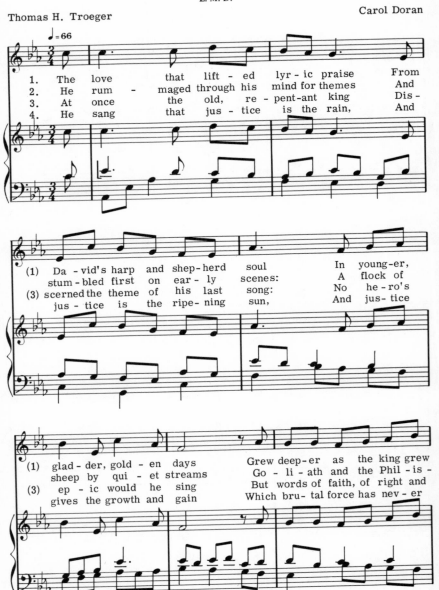

Text based on II Samuel 23: 1-7, especially verses 1, 3-4.

70

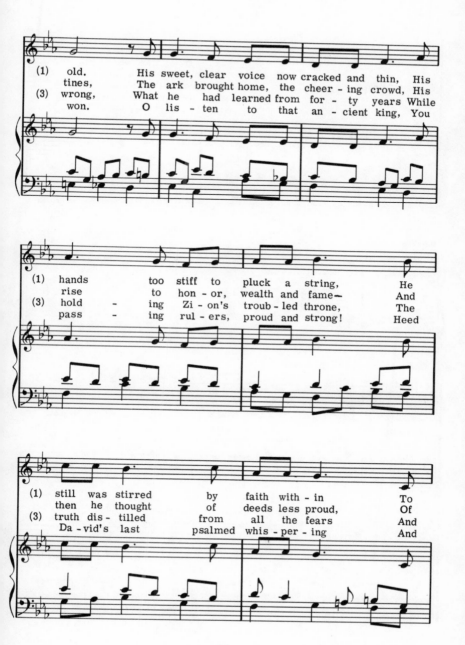

71

(1) write one fi - nal psalm to sing.
pri - vate lust and pub - lic shame.
(3) plots and strug - gles he had known.
live the wis - dom of his song.

Interlude

Optional harmonization for stanza 4.

(4) He sang that jus - tice is the rain, And
jus - tice is the ripe - ning sun, And jus - tice

gives the growth and gain _____ Which bru-tal force has nev-er

won. O lis - ten to that an-cient king, You

pass - ing rul-ers, proud and strong! Heed Da-vid's last psalmed

whis-per-ing And live the wis - dom of his song.

35. How Buoyant and Bold the Stride of Christ's Friends

(tune: Liberation)
10-10-11-11

Thomas H. Troeger

Carol Doran

♩ =126 Slightly stress each downbeat!

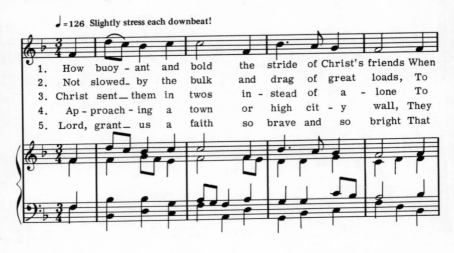

1. How buoy - ant and bold the stride of Christ's friends When
2. Not slowed by the bulk and drag of great loads, To
3. Christ sent them in twos in - stead of a - lone To
4. Ap - proach - ing a town or high cit - y wall, They
5. Lord, grant us a faith so brave and so bright That

(1) swept by his words like high lift - ing winds They
cit - ies and towns, on path - ways and roads, They
(3) tell the good news, wher - ev - er un - known And
won - dered what soul a - wait - ed Christ's call And
(5) we too shall dare to trav - el as light As

Text based on Mark 6: 7-13.

74

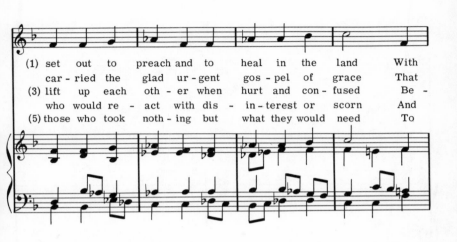

(1) set out to preach and to heal in the land   With
car - ried the glad ur - gent gos - pel of grace   That
(3) lift up each oth - er when hurt and con - fused   Be -
who would re - act with dis - in - terest or scorn   And
(5) those who took noth - ing but what they would need   To

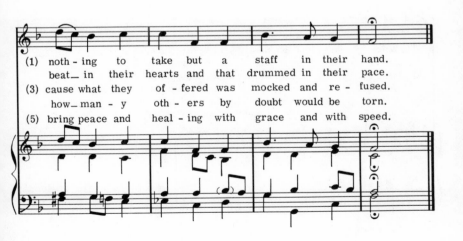

(1) noth - ing to take but a staff in their hand.
beat__ in their hearts and that drummed in their pace.
(3) cause what they of - fered was mocked and re - fused.
how__ man - y oth - ers by doubt would be torn.
(5) bring peace and heal - ing with grace and with speed.

75

36. Wild the Man and Wild the Place

(tune: John Baptist)
7-7-7-7

Thomas H. Troeger

Carol Doran

♩ =108

1. Wild the man and wild the place,
2. "Knock down ev - ery proud backed hill!
3. "Throw your - self in Jor - dan's streams.
4. "Leave on shore un - need - ed weight,
5. "One now comes whose ver - y name
6. "You will see him soon ap - pear:

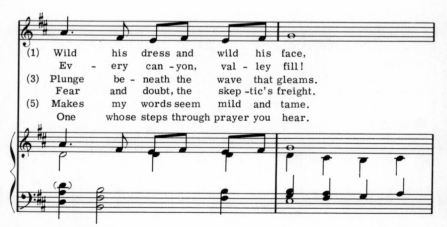

(1) Wild his dress and wild his face,
    Ev - ery can - yon, val - ley fill!
(3) Plunge be - neath the wave that gleams.
    Fear and doubt, the skep -tic's freight.
(5) Makes my words seem mild and tame.
    One whose steps through prayer you hear.

Text based on Mark 1: 1-8.

(1) Wil - der still his words that trace
Plane the soul and pray un - til
(3) Wash a - way what on - ly seems.
Toss them off and do not wait.
(5) I use wa - ter to re - claim
Christ is draw - ing, draw - ing near,

(1) Paths that lead from sin to grace.
All its rau - cous rum - blings still.
(3) Rise and float on heav - en's dreams.
Time is short. The hour is late.
(5) Lives that he will cleanse with flame.
Christ is com - ing, com - ing here!"

1, 2, 3, 4, 5

6

37. Neither Desert Wind nor Sun

(tune: Sister Toinette)
7-7-7-7 D

Thomas H. Troeger

Carol Doran

1. Nei - ther des - ert wind nor sun_____ Nor the
2. Then came dark-ness and a cry:_____ Li - ons
3. Sa - tan's civ - il, rea - soned voice_____ Trav - eled
4. But the bright-er, straight-er beams_____ Shin - ing
5. Lord, O Lord, we know the fear_____ Marked up-
6. In that wild and bar - ren place_____ Where the

(1) wastes of rock and sand_____ Tempt - ed
roar - ing on a hill,_____ Prowl - ing
(3) on the morn - ing breeze:_____ "Why the
from the mid - day sun_____ Swept a -
(5) on the shad - owed sand,_____ Through the
dev - il roams a - bout,_____ Where our

Text based on Mark 1: 12-15.

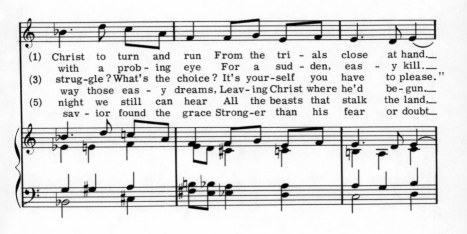

(1) Christ to turn and run From the tri - als close at hand.__
    with a prob - ing eye For a sud - den, eas - y kill.__
(3) strug-gle? What's the choice? It's your-self you have to please."
    way those eas - y dreams, Leav-ing Christ where he'd be-gun.__
(5) night we still can hear All the beasts that stalk the land,__
    sav - ior found the grace Strong-er than his fear or doubt__

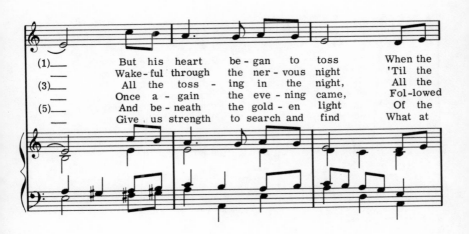

(1)__ But his heart be - gan to toss   When the
    __ Wake-ful through the ner - vous night   'Til the
(3)__ All the toss - ing in the night,   All the
    __ Once a - gain the eve - ning came,   Fol-lowed
(5)__ And be - neath the gold - en light   Of the
    __ Give us strength to search and find   What at

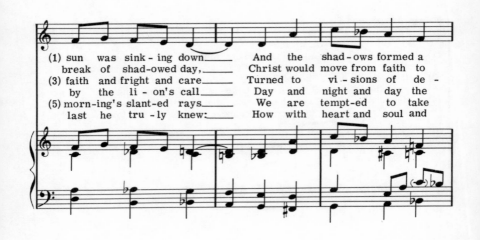

(1) sun   was sink - ing down_____   And   the   shad - ows formed a
    break of   shad-owed day,_____   Christ would move from faith to
(3) faith and fright and care_____   Turned to   vi - sions of   de -
    by   the li - on's call_____   Day   and   night and day the
(5) morn-ing's slant-ed rays_____   We   are   tempt-ed to   take
    last   he   tru - ly knew:_____   How   with heart and soul and

(1) cross   On   the   dead   and bar - ren ground.
    fright, Then shift back   the oth - er   way.
(3) light   In   the   dawn's   de - ceiv - ing air.
    same,   For - ty   days   and nights in   all.
(5) flight From your hard,   de - mand - ing ways.
    mind   We   be - long,   Dear God,   to   you.

80

38. When Heaven's Voice Was Still

(tune: Heaven's Voice)
S. M.

Thomas H. Troeger

Carol Doran

Text based on I Samuel 3: 1-10.

81

39. To Those Who Knotted Nets of Twine

(tune: Storm-swept Way)
C. M.

Thomas H. Troeger

Carol Doran

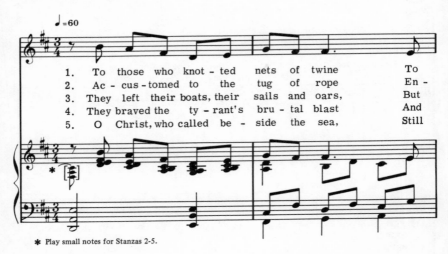

♩ =60

1. To those who knot - ted   nets of twine   To
2. Ac - cus - tomed to the   tug of rope   En -
3. They left their boats, their sails and oars, But
4. They braved the ty - rant's bru - tal blast And
5. O Christ, who called be - side the sea,   Still

* Play small notes for Stanzas 2-5.

(1) comb a fish - filled sea,_____   Christ called a -
    snared in rocks and weeds,_____   They felt from
(3) e - ven more than these,_____   They left the
    hate's un - bound - ed rage,_____ While res - cue
(5) call to us to - day._____   Like those who

Text based on Mark 1: 14-20.

(1) loud: "Put   down   that   line   And come____
    Christ   a   pull   of   hope   A - midst____
(3) lake's   en - cir - cling shores   And its____
    lines   of   faith they   cast   To save____
(5) fished   in   Gal - i - lee,   We'll risk____

1, 2, 3, 4

(1)____ and   fol - low me!"
____ their tan-gled needs.
(3)____ fa - mil - iar breeze.
____ their sink-ing age.

5

(5)____ your storm-swept way.____

83

40. As Servants Working an Estate

(tune: Advent Sunday)
C. M. D.

Thomas H. Troeger   Carol Doran

Text based on Mark 13: 32-37.

84

(1) So none of us can name the hour, The season or the year When Christ with all of heav-en's power Will sud-den-ly ap - pear.

Not load-ing frag-ile hu-man schemes With hopes they can - not bear, We trust the prom-ise that re-deems The pres-ent from de - spair.

(3) Re-veal-ing that the pres-ent age And ev-ery age that's past Are not the fi - nal mor-al gauge That judg-es us at last.

But wel-come you from realms a-bove To your es-tate be-low, Where jus - tice, mer-cy, peace and love A - bun-dant-ly will grow.

41. The Branch That Bends with Clustered Fruit

(tune: Greater Growth)
C. M.

Thomas H. Troeger

Carol Doran

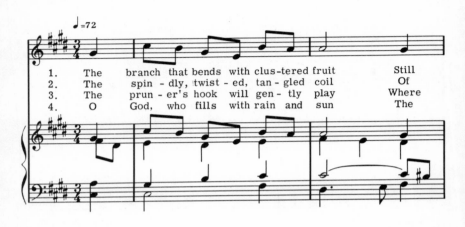

♩=72

1. The branch that bends with clus-tered fruit   Still
2. The spin - dly, twist - ed, tan - gled coil   Of
3. The prun - er's hook will gen - tly play   Where
4. O God, who fills with rain and sun   The

(1) needs   the prun - er's blade   To keep it
     branch - es   o - ver - grown   Pro - duc - es
(3) fruit - ful growth is seen   But like an
     grapes   we press for wine,   Cut off the

Text based on John 15: 1-8.

(1) close to vine and root _____ Or else its
    no - thing from its toil _____ But feeds it -
(3) axe will slash a - way _____ The emp - ty
    growth our fears have spun _____ And prune us

[1, 2, 3,] [4]
(1) strength   will   fade. _____
    self   a -   lone. _____
(3) net   of   green. _____   (4) to   your

(4) vine. _____

87

42. Listen to the Cloud That Brightens

(tune: Bishop Spears)
8-7-8-7 D

Thomas H. Troeger

Carol Doran

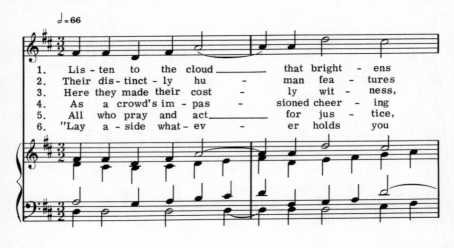

♩ = 66

1. Lis - ten to the cloud _____ that bright - ens
2. Their dis - tinct - ly hu - man fea - tures
3. Here they made their cost - ly wit - ness,
4. As a crowd's im - pas - sioned cheer - ing
5. All who pray and act _____ for jus - tice,
6. "Lay a - side what - ev - er holds you

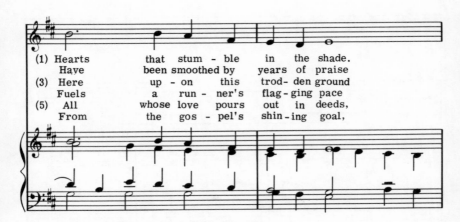

(1) Hearts that stum - ble in the shade.
   Have been smoothed by years of praise
(3) Here up - on this trod- den ground
   Fuels a run - ner's flag - ging pace
(5) All whose love pours out in deeds,
   From the gos - pel's shin - ing goal,

Text based on Colossians 1: 9-14 and Hebrews 12: 1-2.

88

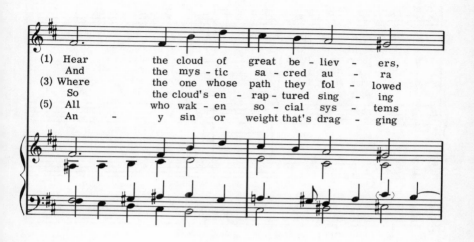

(1) Hear the cloud of great be - liev - ers,
And the mys - tic sa - cred au - ra
(3) Where the one whose path they fol - lowed
So the cloud's en - rap - tured sing - ing
(5) All who wak - en so - cial sys - tems
An - y sin or weight that's drag - ging

(1) Heed the wit - ness they have made:
That en - cir - cles an - cient days,
(3) With a wreath of thorns was crowned.
Streng-thens us to run our race.
(5) To the cry of hu - man needs,
At your heart or mind or soul.

89

(1) Proph-ets who have raged_____ in judg - ment,
Yet those saint-ed ho - ly fig - ures
(3) Now they call from that _____ do - min - ion
We can hear them in _____ our wor - ship,
(5) All who bear their neigh - bor's bur - den,
Fix your eyes a - lone_____ on Je - sus,

(1) Mar-tyrs killed by flame and sword,
Once like us were blood and bone,
(3) Past the range of mor - tal sight,
We can sense them through our prayers,
(5) All who lift the soul that faints,—
Who en - dured the cross and shame,

(1) Bold re - form-ers through the a - ges,
Trou - bled by the same temp-ta - tions,
(3) Joined with Christ in one com-mun - ion
We can see their wit - ness liv - ing
(5) All of these on earth to-geth - er
And press on with per - se-ver - ance

(1) Com - mon folk who loved the Lord.
Doubts and ques - tions we have known.
(3) Of e - ter - nal song and light.
In their brave and faith - ful heirs.
(5) Sing with heav - en's cloud of saints:
For the glo - ry of his name!"

* This interlude may be used between stanzas 5 and 6 by playing the interlude's first measure in place of the tune's last measure and treating the interlude as an extension of the tune.

43. Forever in the Heart There Springs

(tune: Eternal Manna)
L. M. D.

Thomas H. Troeger

Carol Doran

1. For - ev - er in the heart there springs A hun - ger
2. True Bread of Heav - en, Life Di - vine, E - ter - nal
3. Let Christ be praised for - ev - er - more Who makes us

(1) nev - er touched by things, And if un - met, this
    Man - na, Ho - ly Sign, Our need of you in -
(3) rich when we are poor, Who sees the tat - tered,

(1) in - ward need Goes prowl - ing as in - ces - sant greed: _____
    cites our quest, Your pres - ence brings our search to rest: _____
(3) beg - ging soul Be - neath the cloak of class and role, _____

Text based on John 6: 24-35.

92

(1)___ We reach and reach for more and more While
___ The hol - low, hun - gry heart is filled And
(3)___ Who hears the heart's un - spo - ken groan And

(1) with each gain we still seem poor. We work to earn what
all its grasp-ing mo-tions stilled, Our quench-less thirst is
(3) meets our need as if his own, To whom all thirst and

(1) can't be bought; Through prayer and faith it must be sought.
sat - is - fied, And ev - ery need and want sup - plied.
(3) hun - ger yield, The bread whose taste is truth re - vealed.

44. Beyond the Press and Pull of Crowds

(tune: Lonely Place)
C. M.

Thomas H. Troeger

Carol Doran

1. Be - yond the press and pull of
2. The hands which straight-ened an - gled
3. The rag - ged world's raw, rest - less
4. When night at last be - gan to
5. But great - er still, he felt deep
6. Lord, lead us to a lone - ly

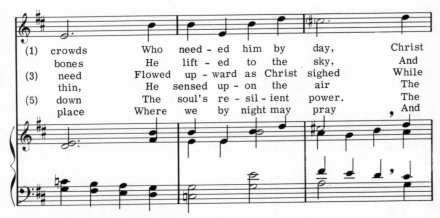

(1) crowds Who need - ed him by day, Christ
    bones He lift - ed to the sky, And
(3) need Flowed up - ward as Christ sighed While
    thin, He sensed up - on the air The
(5) down The soul's re - sil - ient power. The
    place Where we by night may pray, And

Text based on Mark 1: 29-39 (especially verse 35).

94

(1) found   be - neath the moon - rimed clouds   A
     with   the   Spir-it's word - less groans   He
(3) strength   to   heal, to   teach and   feed   The
     bus   -   y   day's ap- proach - ing   din,   Its
(5) lift   of   hope no   grief can   drown   Had
     then,   like   Christ, a - rise to   face   The

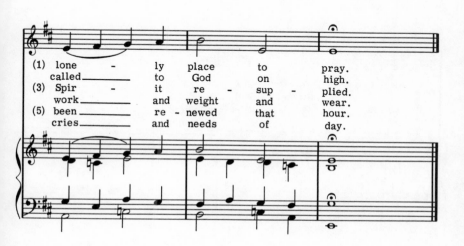

(1) lone   -   ly   place   to   pray.
     called_____ to   God   on   high.
(3) Spir   -   it   re - sup - plied.
     work_____ and   weight and   wear.
(5) been_____ re - newed that   hour.
     cries_____ and   needs   of   day.

45. Let the Truth Shine in Our Speaking

(tune: Heaven's Brightness)
8-7-8-7 D

Thomas H. Troeger

Carol Doran

Text based on Ephesians 4: 25 to 5: 2.

96

(1) As   the pure   and   slant - less stream   -   ing
But   not bear   our   hurt and   an   -   ger
(3) As   we smell   the   pines and   ce   -   dars

(1) Of   the noon's re - veal - ing   ray,
Past the set - ting   of   the   sun.
(3) And the breath - ings of   the   ground,

(1) Wash - ing   earth   in   heav - en's bright - ness
For   our   sin   is   in   our   si   -   lence,
(3) Let Christ's rich   -   er,   mys - tic   fra   -   grance

(1) With the light from straight a - bove,
In the storm that nev - er comes
(3) Rise from hearts this day re - deemed

(1) Then we shall be faith - ful neigh - bors
Or that af - ter - ward still lin - gers
(3) When we spoke the truth as neigh - bors

(1) Linked by Christ's de - ceit - less love.
Sound-ing yet its grum - bling drums.
(3) While the sun - light bright - ly streamed.

46. Far More Than Passion's Passing Flame

(tune: Michael John)
C. M.

Thomas H. Troeger

Carol Doran

1. Far more—than pas-sion's pass-ing flame—Has fused our
2. Through sor - row, joy, temp - ta-tion, strain,—Af - flic- tion,
3. If time—di-lutes what we feel now—And rich de-
4. Then at—our death, O God, ac - cept—This life-long

(1) sin- gle hearts: The vow——— we make in
    rap-ture, tears, Lord, let——— our vows en-
(3) sires— thin, May we——— by grace draw
    gift of praise: The wit - ness of a

(1) heav-en's name One com - mon fu - ture charts.
    dure and gain Their mean - ing through the years.
(3) from our vow The strength to love a - gain.
    prom-ise kept Through all our mar - ried days.

Text based on Mark 10: 2-16.

99

47. Before the Fruit Is Ripened by the Sun

(tune: Renewing Death)
10-10-10-10

Thomas H. Troeger

Carol Doran

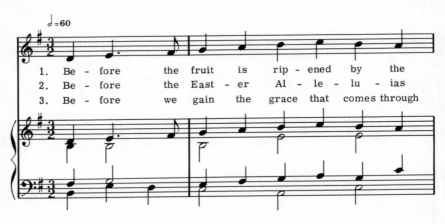

♩=60

1. Be - fore the fruit is rip - ened by the
2. Be - fore the East - er Al - le - lu - ias
3. Be - fore we gain the grace that comes through

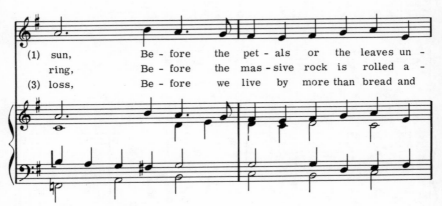

(1) sun, Be - fore the pet - als or the leaves un -
ring, Be - fore the mas - sive rock is rolled a -
(3) loss, Be - fore we live by more than bread and

Text based on John 12: 20-33.

100

(1) coil, Be - fore the first fine silk - en root is
side, Be - fore the fear of death has lost its
(3) breath, Be - fore we lift in joy an emp - ty

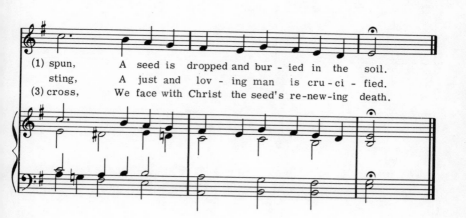

(1) spun, A seed is dropped and bur - ied in the soil.
sting, A just and lov - ing man is cru - ci - fied.
(3) cross, We face with Christ the seed's re - new - ing death.

48. The Moon with Borrowed Light

(tune: Borrowed Light)
S. M. D.

Thomas H. Troeger

Carol Doran

1. The moon with bor-rowed light Gives (1) wit - ness to the sun, Dis-creet-ly fad - ing with the night When morn - ing has be-gun.
2. The tem - ple Le - vites asked What ti - tle did John claim. He said he had a sin - gle task A sin - gle goal and aim:
3. The clouds of sin yet mask Earth's (3) tan - gled, stub-bly ground, And O how man - y hearts still ask Where God's clear path is found.

Text based on John 1: 6-9, 19-28.

(1) John's bor-rowed light was drawn From heav-en's vi-brant rays,—
    To re - di - rect their sight Be - yond what he had done—
(3) For bor-rowed light we pray So we may be a sign—

(1) —— His life a wit - ness to the
(3) —— To Christ the pure and pri - mal
        That points to Christ, the truth, the

(1) dawn Of Christ's ap-proach - ing blaze.
    light That light - ens ev - ery - one.
(3) way, The life, the light di - vine.

49. A Single Unmatched Stone

(tune: Unmatched Stone)
6-6-6-6-8-8

Thomas H. Troeger

Carol Doran

♩=108

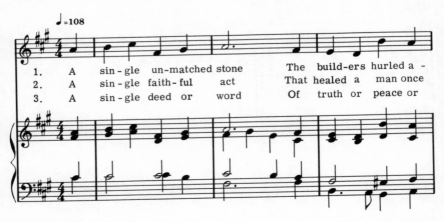

1. A sin-gle un-matched stone   The build-ers hurled a-
2. A sin-gle faith-ful act   That healed a man once
3. A sin-gle deed or word   Of truth or peace or

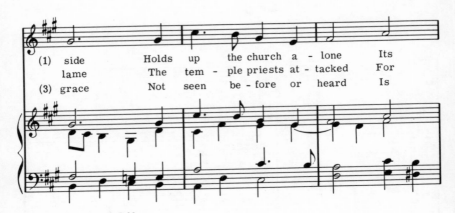

(1) side   Holds up   the church a-lone   Its
lame   The tem-ple priests at-tacked   For
(3) grace   Not seen   be-fore or heard   Is

Text based on Acts 4: 5-12.

104

(1) cor - ner-stone and pride. The sym - me - try the
    bear - ing Je - sus' name. The right-eous heart, the
(3) dif - fi - cult to face. Help us, O God, by

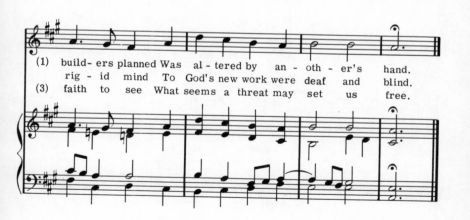

(1) build - ers planned Was al - tered by an - oth - er's hand.
    rig - id mind To God's new work were deaf and blind.
(3) faith to see What seems a threat may set us free.

50. Why Stare at Heaven's Distant Blue

(tune: Waiting)
8-8-8-8-8-8

Thomas H. Troeger

Carol Doran

♩=116

1. "Why stare at heav - en's dis - tant
2. Deep si - lence fell up - on the
3. That con - gre - ga - tion lived be -
4. May we be dis - ci - plined to

(1) blue   When Christ has told you what to do?
    air,   And earth seemed lone - ly, hard and bare,
(3) tween   A well - marked past and things un - seen.
    face   With that young chur - ch's pa - tient grace

(1) __ Your gaze won't draw the clouds back down __
    __ And where Christ's friends had fixed their eyes __
(3) __ With Christ no long - er at their side, __
    __ The prayer - ful, seek - ing, wait - ing days __

Text based on Acts 1: 1-14.

106

(1)— That rose with glo - ry from the ground.
— Stood on - ly sun and cloud and skies.
(3)— Di - rect - ly there to teach and guide,
— That are a part of heav-en's ways,

(1) Your Lord now reigns in realms a - bove. A -
Then with a slow re - luc - tant gait They
(3) They sought through prayer with one ac - cord The
By which we learn how we de - pend On

(1) wait God's wind and show Christ's love."
walked toward home to pray and wait.
(3) will of their as - cend - ed Lord.
God to send the flame and wind.

51. Seek Not in Distant, Ancient Hills

(tune: Sacred Ground)
C. M.

Thomas H. Troeger

Carol Doran

♩ =108

1. Seek not in dis - tant, an - cient
2. A sin - gle heav - en wraps_____ a -
3. To climb the tem - pled, foot ___ worn
4. In spir - it and in truth _____ you'll

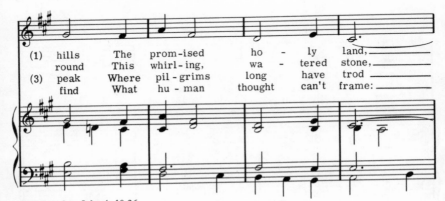

(1) hills The prom - ised ho - ly land, _____
     round This whirl - ing, wa - tered stone, _____
(3) peak Where pil - grims long have trod ___
     find What hu - man thought can't frame: _____

Text based on John 4: 19-26.

(1) But where you live do what ___ God
And ev - ery place is sa - cred
(3) Un - lock the bolt - ed soul ___ and
The source of breath and pulse ___ and

(1) wills And find it ___ close at
ground Where God is ___ loved and
(3) seek The pres - ent, ___ liv - ing
mind, The pri - mal ___ wind and

1, 2, 3   4

(1) hand. ___
known. ___
(3) God. ___   (4) flame. ___

109

52. From Pharaoh to King Cyrus

(tune: Liberation Notes)
7-6-7-6 D

Thomas H. Troeger

Carol Doran

1. From Phar - aoh to King Cy - rus___ To Al - ex-
2. Their pal - ac - es have crum - bled,___ Their scep-ters,
3. Let ty - rants and their min - ions___ Who plot how
4. Clear notes of lib - er - a - tion___ Are trill - ing
5. Christ's high rhap - sod - ic vi - sion___ Of truth and

(1) an - der's reign ___ To Cae - sar's PAX RO -
crowns and thrones, ___ And where their ar - mies
(3) they will bend ___ The world to be their
in our hearts; ___ They are the pulse of
(5) love and peace ___ Has loos - ened dreams and

(1) MAN - A There marched a haugh - ty
rum - bled The soil is chalk from
(3) ser - vants Hear Christ who calls us
con - science Our daunt - less friend im -
(5) yearn - ings That will not fade or

Text based on John 15: 9-17, especially 14-15.

© 1985, Oxford University Press, Inc.

110

(1) train   Of po - ten-tates and des - pots   Each
    bones.   Thus Pon - tius Pi - late's van -ished Who
(3)"friend."   No threat from mod - ern Cae - sars,   No
    parts,   The quick - ened beat for jus - tice   That
(5) cease.   We fear no earth - ly pow - er   For

(1) act - ing   as   a   god,   De - mand-ing praise and
    wield- ed   Cae - sar's sword,   Yet lives the one he
(3) or - der   to   o - bey   What con - tra-dicts the
    thick - ens tim - id blood,   Sup - ply-ing us with
(5) we   are   claimed as friends   By that all - gra - cious

(1) hom - age___ From ev - ery   land   they   trod.
    ban -ished:___ Our ris - en, reign - ing   Lord!
(3) gos - pel ___ Shall turn us   from   Christ's   way.
    cour - age___ To stem earth's vio - lent   flood.
(5) rul - er___ Whose king-dom nev - er   ends.

111

Metrical Index

Scriptural Index

114

115

Index by Theme and Image

BOLDNESS OF BELIEF

BUILDING (CHURCH'S PHYSICAL PLANT)

CALL TO FAITH AND MINISTRY

CHRISTMAS

CHURCH

123

Index of Hymns in Sequence
for the Liturgical Year

These hymns are based on the lessons for Year B in the common lectionary which enjoys wide ecumenical use in the churches of North America. However, a number of the lessons for high holy days are the same each year and can be used for A and C cycles as well. For example, Pentecost Sunday always includes the reading of Acts 2: 1-13 on which "Wind Who Makes All Winds That Blow" is based. Also, many of the hymns will make excellent liturgical sense even when the lection is not being read. You may find it helpful to check the Index by Theme and Image for different portions of your service, such as praise, prayer, worship, and so on.

Since lectionary resources sometimes vary in how they assign lessons after Pentecost, you may find slight discrepancies in the sequence of lessons following Trinity Sunday, and you may have to count forward or backward one Sunday from the order given here.

There are four hymns marked with an asterisk, indicating that these lessons were part of the ecumenical lectionary the poet used though they are not found in the common lectionary.

2nd Sunday	When Heaven's Voice Was Still	38
3rd Sunday	To Those Who Knotted Nets of Twine	39
4th Sunday	Silence! Frenzied, Unclean Spirit	25
5th Sunday	Beyond the Press and Pull of Crowds	44
6th Sunday	The Leper's Soul Was No Less Scarred	26
7th Sunday	Gangling Desert Birds Will Sing	16
7th Sunday	We Have the Strength to Lift and Bear	28

(*Note:* We cover both the Old Testament and gospel lections because each is a very popular text for preachers.)

LENT

1st Sunday	Neither Desert Wind nor Sun	37
2nd Sunday	The Lick of the Tide, the Lunge of the Storm*	18
3rd Sunday	Seek Not in Distant, Ancient Hills (based on the Gospel for Year A)	51
4th Sunday	A Spendthrift Lover Is the Lord	12
5th Sunday	Before the Fruit Is Ripened by the Sun	47
Palm Sunday	A Cheering, Chanting, Dizzy Crowd	22

EASTER

Easter Sunday	No Iron Spike, No Granite Weight	32
2nd Sunday	These Things Did Thomas Count as Real	33
3rd Sunday	Too Splendid for Speech but Ripe for a Song*	8
4th Sunday	A Single Unmatched Stone	49
5th Sunday	The Branch That Bends with Clustered Fruit	41
6th Sunday	From Pharaoh to King Cyrus	52
Ascension Day (or Sunday after if observed then)	Why Stare at Heaven's Distant Blue	50

PENTECOST

Pentecost Sunday	Wind Who Makes All Winds That Blow	11
1st Sunday (Trinity)	Suddenly God's Sovereign Wind	10
2nd Sunday	Unless This Day Be Holy*	5
3rd Sunday	If Christ Is Charged with Madness	29
4th Sunday	The First Day of Creation	14
5th Sunday	The Sails Were Spilling Wind	31
6th Sunday	The Scantest Touch of Grace Can Heal	24

Index of First Lines

ISBN   0 19 385729